The Playwright

"There are seven subjects
best avoided on television."

— Dennis Benge

The Playwright

Daren White - story
Eddie Campbell - art

Top Shelf Productions
Knockabout Comics

The Scenes

6 On the bus

26 Online

46 In the park

50 At school

64 On the continent

80 Incontinent

98 Appendix

116 An accounting

134 The actor

142 Curtain

Scene One
On the bus

The playwright often considers other people who, along with him, employ public transport.

The young girl opposite is wearing a rather fetching white cotton blouse.

Marks and Spencer by the look of it.

You can see where the buttons are starting to pull across the chest.

The thing is, she's put on a bit of weight since then.

She probably bought it when she got her first job.

Two lovely big juicy dumplings trying to break out and brighten up the day.

The playwright's first impulse is to head straight home and lock himself in the bathroom for five minutes.

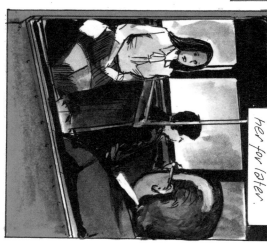

But he calms himself and makes a mental note to save her for later.

He loved the way her hair smelled of marzipan.

With whom he struck up a friendship in the local stationers'.

The playwright once dated a much younger girl

and found her ever-so-slightly crossed eyes strangely attractive.

In the parlor of her grandmother's council house, he thought his chance had come.

But he choked and fumbled and fled with embarrassment, never speaking to her again.

But he couldn't be sure.

He thought he might have caught her eye.

He passed the girl in the street, years later.

The playwright spends a large portion of his day thinking about love and sex.

His 1985 award-winning screenplay, "An Ambiance of Nicotine and Stewed Tea" was based upon the reflections of his missed opportunities.

The playwright never wastes good material.

He planned the exercise with military precision.

The playwright once visited a local prostitute.

But on the day, he couldn't rid himself of a nagging thought.

The number of times she would have lain there soaking up sperm.

And he found himself unable to perform.

Ernie's real family have long since passed away.

The playwright lodges in Uncle Ernie's spare room.

20

It was his own mother's birthday last week but he didn't send her a card.

His 1978 award-winning screenplay, "The Secret," was largely based upon his older, retarded brother.

And the playwright hasn't been welcome since it aired.

But he never wastes good material.

The playwright regrets this loss of family.

Never. Ever.

The playwright returns home to collate the notes he has mentally formed during the day.

As the kettle boils, he thinks he can see the formation of a new idea.

He'll soon begin the first draft.

Scene Two
Online

28

The price of quality footwear has risen greatly in comparison to inflation over the years, but the playwright considers the cost of shabbiness far higher.

Unlike the tradesman who delivers his new personal computer.

Although new to home computing, the playwright is confident that the word processing features will prove useful.

The playwright prides himself that his work appeals across the generations.

And he feels glad that he is still in touch with modern technology.

Within a short period of time, the playwright has become quite obsessed with Internet pornography.

In his younger years he might have purchased the occasional girlie magazine but had no real exposure to hardcore material.

He considers himself wise in the ways of the world but is shocked by some of the images he finds.

The playwright rarely ventures past the introductory menu pages.

Not so much because he doesn't want to pay the access fee...

But rather he feels that he would be lowering his standards.

However, he still spends hours searching the internet for new sites...

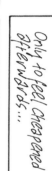

Only to feel cheapened afterwards...

At the waste of his valuable time.

His success over the years has made him an important Client, and he feels that an occasional lunch is the least he deserves.

The playwright makes a monthly visit to his agent's office.

He isn't overly indulgent by nature, but on such occasions he always orders the finest wine.

The playwright's agent is an attractive lady some fifteen years his junior, and for years he has believed himself to be in love with her.

Although she has accompanied him to a number of industry award evenings, he has never made a romantic advance toward her.

The fiancé found this quite amusing.

Prior to the agent's marriage, some ten years ago, the playwright felt it appropriate to assure her fiancé that there had never been an improper element to their relationship.

He admires her lovely bone structure and thinks her magnificent jaw line has only been improved by time and a finesse of fine lines.

During one such visit to his agent's office, one of the young secretaries was showing her newly born daughter.

The playwright was not particularly interested in the baby and was somewhat distracted by how much the young mother's breasts had grown.

She had been very slim before falling pregnant and had already regained her prenatal waist, which was accentuated by her more than ample bosom.

As the baby was passed round the office, an unexpected anxiety manifested itself within him.

While not a young man, he still feels that his best years lie ahead of him and that he has much to offer a young wife and family.

The playwright never really cared much for children, but still took solace from the fact that Charlie Chaplin fathered a child in his eighties.

The playwright was overcome by the notion that if the were passed the baby he would throw it out the nearest window.

He was horrified that such a thought could enter his mind and took a precaution of step toward the center of the room.

Fortunately, the baby stirred before reaching him and was passed back to its mother.

Since Uncle Ernie's death, the playwright often spends his days without human contact.

He can easily afford cable television but prefers the social interaction provided by the public house.

The playwright often watches the live broadcast of Premier League football matches at the Treacle Pot.

And his critically lauded drama 'Tea for One' was written during this period of sadness.

After patronising the pub for a number of months, the bar staff occasionally greet him upon his entrance.

And other locals pass remark about the game.

He feels an acceptance long since bleached out of him by his public school education, national service, career, solitude and family rejection.

Although he knows better than to confuse such acquaintance with genuine friendship.

The playwright regards this as a great breakthrough in his social conditioning.

The playwright always sleeps on his back.

Since reading an article about strangulated testicles he has never been comfortable with the way his testicles hang when laying on his side.

An unexpected twist in the night could mean the loss of progeny within a matter of minutes.

A minor character in his award-winning drama 'Rainy Like Sunday Morning' was based upon 'Wombie' Davis...

...an unfortunate pupil from his school days who had found the ball in a match-day rugby scrum but lost something far more valuable.

After a boggling few hours, the playwright resigns himself to a sleepless night.

44

As he reaches for his dressing gown he feels the first few pangs of guilt.

And he mentally chastises himself as he makes his way downstairs toward the computer.

Ignoring the self-loathing, he logs onto the pregnancy.com website and types 'breasts' into the search engine.

Scene Three
In the park

He once saw a pigeon defecate on to a businessman's shoulder.

It's a good place to mentally sort his ideas and is often frequented by pretty young ladies.

The playwright rather enjoys a quiet moment in the park.

It strikes him as absurd that such an event is often considered lucky.

Surely the luck lies with passers by who, statistically, are far less likely to be similarly soiled at that precise moment.

In the same way, the playwright always derives an almost perverse sense of relief whenever he receives news that an old friend has developed prostate cancer.

And to be honest, at his age his prostate needs all the statistical support he can muster.

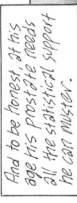

Because statistically, he reasons such news significantly reduces the danger of him being similarly afflicted.

Scene Four
At school

He assumes that vanity is playing a role, which seems odd, considering the woman's age, obesity and fashion sense.

The playwright is rarely a victim to vanity, although he was somewhat alarmed when his hairline began to fail while still in his early thirties.

However, he considered it absurd to fret excessively over an uncontrollable imperfection when he was riddled with a number of other aberrations.

The playwright had been a clever child.

A high pass at the eleven-plus examination had secured a scholarship for a nearby school of fine repute.

The playwright's retarded older brother required constant attention and so his family had opted for him to board at the school.

And years later he would identify this single decision as the root of his inability to form close social relationships.

He immediately struggled with the sudden immersion in such a strict and loveless environment.

56

His award-winning TV series, Crack for Crack, might ostensibly have been an examination of the connection between Cocaine prostitution and Kings Cross railway station...

However, more than one critic noted that many of the wretched characters had their fate apparently determined by a loss of family security.

For some time he had suspected that he was not isolated in his pleasure of the palm. However, at such a fragile age, he could imagine nothing worse than honesty.

During his first week in the dormitory, the playwright was shocked by the other boys' open attitude to masturbation.

The playwright was also shocked by the maturity of the older boys.

His was not a family at ease with the naked body.

And beyond the occasional glimpse of his brother, he had no basis upon which to form comparison.

...his first few terms might have proven unbearable.

And were it not for the persistent bedwetting of the unfortunately named Pryke...

The playwright's own sexual immaturity often made him the unfortunate target of the prefects' bullying.

The playwright's bed was situated next to that of a young lad who couldn't be classified as an obsessive self-abuser...

...but who would, on random occasions, awake in the small hours and frantically pleasure himself, with little regard for the other boys.

The playwright learned that, on such occasions, his classmate had slept awkwardly upon his arm and awoken with it completely numbed.

The playwright adopted the practice himself.

This technique became popular within the dormitory and was known as "greeting the stranger."

His technique was to finish himself off before the onset of pins-and-needles.

In fact, he came to consider it one of the few invaluable lessons learned during this period of schooling.

In later life, he would deliberately attempt to beckon the stranger by purposely sleeping on his right hand...

...such that the stranger eventually became no stranger at all.

Scene Five

On the Continent

He reasons that an obese but pretty young lady would be far more likely to judge him favourably.

And the increased popularity of weight-loss programs leads to the germination of a new scheme.

The Playwright commits a large percentage of his time to formulating new methods for meeting women.

And she may possibly feel obliged to return his affection after his support for her during an extensive weight-loss program.

The playwright attends a weight-loss clinic focus group to survey potential targets.

However, nerves and an inevitable lack of confidence stifle any chance of striking up a conversation.

but is definitely somewhat relaxed around the middle.

He is by no means obese...

Ironically, the playwright soon becomes concerned with his own physique.

He is alarmingly conscious that some potential young wife...

might expect an illuminated room...

during conjugal relations.

And an inspiring deluge of new ideas.

The playwright is soon immersed in a fascinating new culture and is surprised at both his enjoyment...

The playwright has noted the popularity of gymnasium membership among young people and joins a local establishment.

With newfound confidence, the playwright arranges his first summer holiday in more than a decade.

Soon he's aboard a flight to the Mediterranean island of Cyprus.

The playwright completed two years of national service on the island during the 1950s.

He found the restrictive routine of monotony and boredom exhausting and futile.

The Suez Crisis was still to happen, but the playwright could see the writing on the wall for the 'Empire'.

He was unable to appreciate the island's beauty then due to strict curfews resulting from anti-colonial violence.

The Playwright also despised this second period of dormitory accommodation...

Although he did find the other servicemens nightly practice of comparing sticky fingers strangely nostalgic.

PRIVATE'S
PRIVATES
by DENNIS BENGE

The Playwright was not yet of legal drinking age and lamented that his preferred soft drink was unavailable on the island at this time.

In fact, from the time he was discharged and returned to Britain, the playwright was never directly employed again.

By the time he completed his second year, he had generated sufficient funds to finance a full-time writing career.

With customary diligence, he soon established himself as the beverage importation agent and within six months was supplying branded soft drink to the whole of Cyprus.

Halfway through the second week of his holiday, the playwright falls into conversation with a wealthy lady similarly aged to himself.

The lady is quite knowledgeable about his work and seems genuinely interested in a number of his personal anecdotes.

The playwright's low personal confidence usually renders him too embarrassed to interact with female fans of his work.

and that while continuing her husband's business and raising her daughter, has never found the time for romance.

The couple dines together for three consecutive nights and he learns that she was widowed quite early in life...

However the lady's enthusiasm places him at ease and his conversation sparkles in a manner that usually evades him.

On the final evening of his holiday, the playwright plans to invite the Lady to accompany him to an upcoming awards ceremony.

The ceremony will include a silver service supper and he will book an overnight room at the five-star venue.

The Lady lives far enough outside the capital to justify spending the night.

However, as he waits for her to join him at the bar, he overhears a group of men discussing the Lady's bikini line.

And so he will reserve the adjoining suite to accommodate all potential outcomes.

He is horrified when one of the men boasts that she offered to perform fellatio on him.

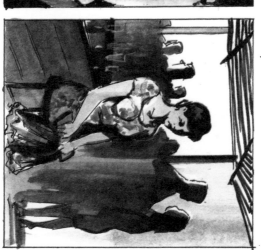

The playwright never speaks to the Lady again.

Scene Six
Incontinent

82

The playwright's parents die within a matter of months of each other, and his retarded older brother has no one to care for him.

... preferring instead to engage a residential nurse at his home, and convert the study into a crèche.

Although financially comfortable, the playwright decides against placing his retarded older brother in a commercial nursing establishment...

The playwright had not made peace with his mother before she died and suffers tremendous guilt during his time of grieving.

The playwright is surprisingly contented by this first real family contact since Uncle Ernie's passing a number of years earlier.

The nurse is a middle-aged spinster who spent much of her adult life caring for her recently departed mother.

The mother had been widowed at an early age and used various ailments over the years to prevent her nurse from leaving home.

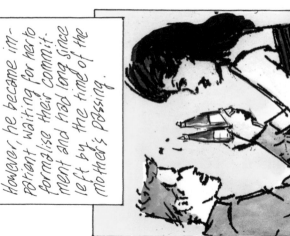

However, he became impatient waiting for her to formalise their commitment and had long since left by the time of the mother's passing.

The nurse had once been engaged to a secondhand book dealer to whom she was introduced by a kindly relative.

During her formative years, the nurse was discouraged from bringing friends into the house and had to submit to a strict curfew when socialising.

The nurse's father had been fastidious about bathroom cleanliness, such that he once refused to use the communal toilet block during a long weekend holiday camp.

By the time the family returned home he was badly constipated and needed a loosening enema at the local hospital.

The relief was instant. However, he experienced a final flourish during the tram ride home.

At least he was spared the indignity of soiled underpants, which most witnesses assumed was the result of the shock.

He was struck by a passing goods vehicle and died instantly.

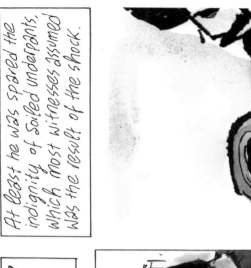

He jumped off in panic before the tram had reached its stop.

The nurse has performed many bowel evacuations in her career and is never as resentful of the procedure as many of her colleagues.

She sometimes wonders if this is in some way connected to her father, but always dismisses it as silly.

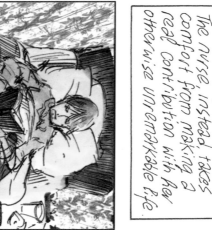

The nurse, instead, takes comfort from making a real contribution with her otherwise unremarkable life.

The playwright conscientiously subscribes to a number of women's magazines to keep in touch with contemporary issues facing the modern girl...

...and is somewhat intrigued to learn that the 21 to 30 decile prefer their partners circumcised.

The playwright wants to appear a considerate lover and, for a while, considers a voluntary medical procedure.

89

However, he is intimidated by the notion that the nursing staff might judge his anesthetized penis...

...and resolves instead to pay particular attention to genital cleanliness during his morning bath.

...which, ironically, turns out to have been authored by a middle-aged man.

The playwright's award-winning teleplay, 'Nice Chap', generously credits its inspiration to the original article...

The playwright's retarded older brother is incontinent and also fond of rubbing himself against various objects around the house.

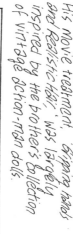

His movie treatment, 'Gripping Hands and Realistic Hair,' was largely inspired by the brother's collection of vintage action-man dolls.

The brother has an uncanny knack of defecating during meals, and the playwright feels sympathetic to young families with untrained infants.

He is embarrassed that the nurse has to experience such occurrences and tremendously admires her silent fortitude when addressing the clean-up.

93

Scene Seven
Appendix

100

The playwright prides himself on the regularity of his daily motion.

which he largely credits to a healthy diet and long walks.

In fact during a playful moment of self-mockery, he often imagines himself pitching an autobiographical skit titled *Regular as Clockwork*.

The playwright's usual doctor is away on annual leave and his locum is a rather attractive lady in her late thirties.

The playwright is rendered speechless when she requests that he drop his trousers...

to allow her to perform a rectal examination.

102

The Locum does not detect any trapped stool, but is nonetheless concerned about a stabbing pain above the right groin.

She recommends plenty of fluids and recounts an amusing anecdote concerning an elderly patient who was constipated and had diarrhea at the same time.

He is later awoken in the middle of the night by excruciating pain and collapses on the way to the bathroom.

And he marks the occasion with a nice glass of aged semillon.

The playwright is relieved when his usual constitution resumes that evening.

Fortunately his brother's nurse hears his crying and suspecting appendicitis immediately calls an ambulance.

Within the hour the playwright lies medicated in a preoperative suite while an Australian male nurse,

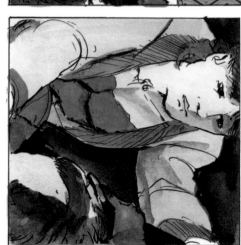

ironically born near the vineyard that made the nice Semillon, shaves his pubic hair.

when the doctor explains
that the complaint is
quite rare in a man of
his age.

He spends three nights in
hospital and bizarrely
feels almost special...

The nurse correctly surmises
that the playwright's appendix
is perforated and an emergency
operation is performed.

A self-administering morphine drip is connected during the first twenty-four hours.

And the playwright is elated at the ease with which he can blank his mind.

However, he fears that the wall-mounted television is plotting to steal his next script.

to the 'Memoirs of a Slave Princess' genre, tentatively titled 'They Stitched me up.'

Immediately prior to his dis- charge, the playwright gathers notes for a stream-of- consciousness approach...

He is secretly relieved the following day when a nurse informs him that oral pain relief will now suffice.

108

Clarity resumes and he
quickly abandons the
idea as foolhardy.

And spends the best part
of the following fortnight
in bed.

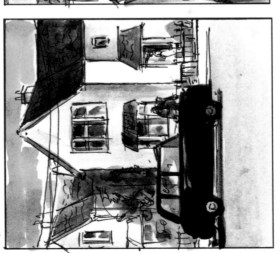

The playwright returns home
under the care of his
brother's nurse.

The nurse tells the playwright that he is well enough to resume normal activities.

He thanks her most genuinely for her support throughout this particularly difficult period.

In truth, the nurse has quite enjoyed taking charge of the household and appreciates the fiduciary relationship with which she is entrusted.

the nurse counter-suggests that they might dine out one evening.

But if arrangements can be made for the Playwright's retarded older brother,

The Playwright suggests that they celebrate, thinking of uncorking one of his special bottles.

The Playwright half recalls the nurse kissing him good night...

He assumes the incident ocurred in a dream.

a few days before.

But now he wonders if he was mistaken.

A few weeks later the nurse accompanies the playwright to his favourite restaurant.

As they are directed to his usual table, he feels a vice-like grip of anxiety.

Which worsens once he realizes that his favourite waitress will be attending to their table.

As the evening progresses, the playwright is surprised to find himself increasingly relaxed.

And his generous tip at the end of the meal is a good indication of how much he has enjoyed the experiance.

The nurse thanks him with a kiss on the cheek.

The Playwright reflects that he has not once had to abruptly avert his stare from the waitress' chest during the entire evening.

Scene Eight
An accounting

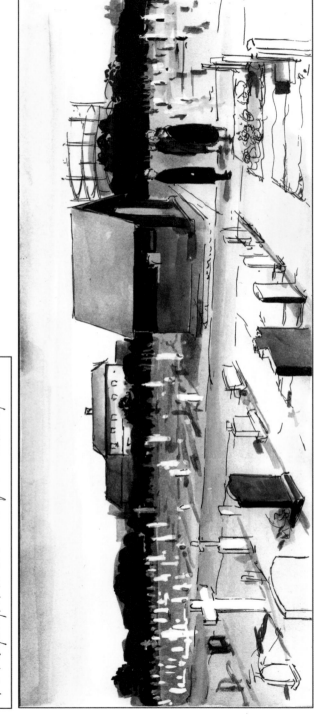

The playwright's brother dies quite suddenly.

A chest infection led to pneumonia.

And within weeks it is over.

The nurse notifies a few distant cousins and attends to the funeral details with customary diligence.

The Playwright mourns his brother but, if challenged, would confess that it is more out of duty than from real emotional trauma.

He sits alone for hours in his favourite restaurant, nursing a 1975 Y'quem and a ripe peach...

But he cannot shed a tear.

A few days later the Playwright watches a late-night documentary that interviews clever children from poor backgrounds, and follows their lives at intervals.

He is intrigued by the subject, hoping to glimpse a familiarity with his own upbringing.

He qualifies this so far as to say that he isn't so much jealous of his former peers' financial success as he resents their lack of creativity in enjoying it.

The lad reflects upon his lack of interest, discipline, and fiscal ambition, then concludes that while he considers himself happy, he covets disposable wealth.

However, he is stung by the commentary of an East-end market trader who excelled in school before dropping out.

As the camera pulls back to show his young family playing in the back garden of their tiny, pre-war terraced house...

The playwright suddenly bursts into tears.

The honest self-appraisal releases a torrent of emotion of such intensity that he sobs for hours.

He wonders whether he is depressed, but is in fact quite contented around the house and enjoys the break from his relentless (mental) narration.

While many of his ideas are quickly discarded he normally spends a few hours every day recording his thoughts.

The playwright doesn't write another word for over three weeks, which is very unusual.

The playwright dines out with the nurse most weekends.

And he realizes that their trips to cinema and theatre are also becoming a welcome habit.

He is startled one night by an erotic dream featuring his brother and the nurse, and is surprised by the implication.

And such an image would normally commandeer his nocturnal subconscious.

Surprised not so much because such a dream is untypical, but rather because he spotted an open house during a recent stroll.

The playwright visits his accountant to execute some financial documents.

The man had been a contestant on a TV game show some thirty years earlier, and had been thoroughly beaten by a hackney cab driver and a fragile spinster from some dreary seaside town.

SMYTHE

In fact the accountant has been carrying on a secret affair with his secretary over the last fifteen years.

He assumed that the man's lack of social grace derived from this humiliation.

The playwright has always felt superior to the accountant...

128

The irony is that the secretary isn't married, but they have conducted the relationship illicitly just to add a little extra excitement.

The playwright observes the pair glance at each other while she serves the tea and biscuits, and their secret seems blatantly obvious.

He feels like a dunce for being oblivious to the charade, but experiences a vicarious thrill at the delicious nature of their deceit.

The nurse is worried that the passing of the playwright's brother will result in the redundancy of her services.

She is surprised at how cozy their lives have become and enjoys the increasingly frequent outings.

She still refers to him as Mr. Benge, although more as a shared joke than to stand on ceremony, and he has called her Patricia for quite some time.

The nurse is, however, relieved when he formalizes the nature of her employment.

And while 'housekeeper' sounds somewhat old-fashioned...

She is horrified to think that she might otherwise be judged a kept woman.

By highlighting the financial windfall she has enjoyed by managing the playwright over the last decade.

In fact, the nurse allows herself an uncharacteristically capricious moment when she embarrasses the agent ...

She is not concerned that the time he spends writing has recently dwindled, but is aware that his agent is becoming cold towards her as each successive deadline is missed.

A few months later, the playwright is still not writing with any frequency.

He finds it increasingly difficult to shake the notion that a lifetime of loneliness has been the seed of his creativity.

The playwright once took great pride in the many literary and media awards that he won.

who naively traded happiness for commercial success.

The playwright is still proud of his body of work, but resents the choices he made as a young man...

But lately he realizes that many of those awards have probably never even been heard of by the public at large.

Scene Nine
The actor

The actor arranges a thank-you dinner at an exclusive London restaurant, the chef of which is well known from an explosive fly-on-the-wall TV documentary.

It is sufficiently successful that the lead actor has been courted by a major Hollywood producer.

The playwright's award-winning stage play, 'Tea for One', has recently been adapted to film.

Kusholme Ruffians

The actor is best known in the industry for being extremely well endowed.

Consequently he is very willing to include full-frontal nudity in much of his work.

In fact, were the playwright to ghostwrite the man's autobiography, he would probably title it 'The Right Part for the Part.'

136

Most of which centre on his famous part, playfully referred to as "Bonaparte".

He mesmerizes both the playwright's agent and the nurse, with many humorous anecdotes...

The actor is most charming in the flesh.

The playwright notices that both women kissed him full on the lips when saying goodnight.

During the taxi ride home the nurse comments that he appeared much taller in real life than on the screen.

This observation seems odd, given that they all spent most of the evening sitting.

As an analogy for his more
intimate physiology.

It occurs to him that the nurse
may be using the actor's height...

The playwright experiences a
bout of insomnia.

However, a late-night internet search confirms that both men are in fact identical in height.

It also turns up considerable evidence suggesting that the actor is a closet homosexual.

Taking comfort from this information he drifts off to sleep.

Scene Ten
Curtain

Oddly enough, of his many creative ventures, it is the playwright's long-held interest in saucy seaside postcards that comes closest to being revived.

Nurse!
NO!
I said
PRICK
his
BOIL

George Orwell's essay about Donald McGill piqued his interest as a youth and he has often considered writing an extensive text on the subject.

But there's many a slip between c cup and lip, mister.

Our honeymoon is off to a start, but I
don't think it's going to be long enough.

In fact, the playwright's first
professional sales were
single-gag ideas which
he sold to a novelty
publisher after returning
home from his
national service.

146

The publisher subsequently requested more explicit material for syndication to a range of gentlemen's magazines, but he declined the offer fearing that sexual inexperience would eventually trip him up.

"Sergeant, that's the one that flashed me. I'd recognise that thing anywhere."

He retrieved the typewriter from the attic and spent three weeks locating an enthusiast experienced in servicing his 1950's model.

His most original idea in months was to attempt to write his new story on the original typewriter he had used at the start of his career.

The playwright stares at the blank page for almost an hour before concluding that he has nothing to say.

None of which has altered the fact that without any financial dependency, crippling self-judgement...

or an optimistic hope of impressing estranged family members...

the playwright has absolutely nothing left to say.

While spending a penny, the playwright notices a young man contemplating the prophylactic vending machine.

The nurse and the playwright are enjoying an evening drink at the Treacle Pot.

THE TREACLE POT

The teenage lad is clearly embarrassed. The playwright gives him an encouraging nod, largely because he also faces the same daunting challenge.

The playwright feels a connection with his newly established kinsman and finds himself ordering the same bottle of imported lager as his young peer.

This should have tipped off the nurse that something is afoot, because he is strictly a wine drinker.

The production company preparing his new television series is threatening to withdraw finance if draft manuscripts are not delivered soon.

A wet Tuesday morning brings correspondence from the playwrights agent.

The playwright assembled the proposal in an hour at home alone, during the nurse's recent visit to a gallery opening.

The nurse returned with a gift of a small original McGill sketch...

Stunning the playwright with the gift's perfection intimacy, and, no doubt, fiscal value.

The playwright has a notion that a driving holiday through the Champagne region will make a nice Easter break.

The thought of a formally organized excursion renders him somewhat uneasy.

And so, there on the spot...

He decides
to learn
to drive.

He is immediately filled
with a sense of excitement,

mentally picturing the
car he will drive.

156

The playwright was surprised by a bright-orange young girl on the bus earlier today...

who he assumed must have self-administered one of those fake tans which are apparently quite fashionable.

He chuckles to himself in recognition of how little he understands the younger generation.

The Playwright has reached his conclusion...

And he never writes another word.

Eddie Campbell and Daren White are expatriate Britons living in Brisbane, Australia. They first met in 1993.

Campbell's credits include the hefty tomes FROM HELL (with Alan Moore), ALEC: THE YEARS HAVE PANTS and A DISEASE OF LANGUAGE (with Alan Moore), as well as the full-color books THE FATE OF THE ARTIST, THE BLACK DIAMOND DETECTIVE AGENCY and THE AMAZING REMARKABLE MONSIEUR LEOTARD.

Daren White is the editor of the Australian anthology, DEEVEE. He has written for a number of Australian publications, including Campbell's BACCHUS magazine, and for DC and Dark Horse Comics in the US. He is also a Chartered Accountant.

The two have worked together on a numbers of projects, including GOTHAM EMERGENCY and BATMAN: THE ORDER OF BEASTS, which was Campbell's first full-color book.